YOUR KNOWLEDGE HAS VALUE

Sarah Ruhnau

The Concept of Femininity in Old English Saints' Lives

The Lives of Pelagia of Antioch and Mary of Egypt

GRIN Verlag

Bibliografische Information der Deutschen Nationalbibliothek:

Die Deutsche Bibliothek verzeichnet diese Publikation in der Deutschen National-
bibliografie; detaillierte bibliografische Daten sind im Internet über http://dnb.d-
nb.de/ abrufbar.

Imprint:

Copyright © 2012 GRIN Verlag GmbH
Druck und Bindung: Books on Demand GmbH, Norderstedt Germany
ISBN: 978-3-656-51546-3

This book at GRIN:

http://www.grin.com/en/e-book/262764/the-concept-of-femininity-in-old-english-
saints-lives

GRIN - Your knowledge has value

Der GRIN Verlag publiziert seit 1998 wissenschaftliche Arbeiten von Studenten, Hochschullehrern und anderen Akademikern als eBook und gedrucktes Buch. Die Verlagswebsite www.grin.com ist die ideale Plattform zur Veröffentlichung von Hausarbeiten, Abschlussarbeiten, wissenschaftlichen Aufsätzen, Dissertationen und Fachbüchern.

Visit us on the internet:

http://www.grin.com/

http://www.facebook.com/grincom

http://www.twitter.com/grin_com

A Holy Harlot?

An Observation of Femininity in OE Female Saint's Lives

In the following essay the concept of femininity in Old English female saint's lives will be examined and analysed. Due to the brevity of this essay, only two saint's lives will be investigated, the Life of Mary of Egypt and Pelagia of Antioch. Both of them are often referred to as 'harlot saints' because of their not only promiscuous but also highly sinful lives before becoming their pious selves. (cf. Cox Miller) It is therefore very interesting that both do not only avert themselves from their previous lives, but even find religious patrons who become ardent worshippers of these women. There are two main aspects which I will focus on in this essay. Considering that women did not receive much appreciation in Old English times in general, it is even more striking that these saints were not just any women, but prostitutes of the most extreme kind. Possible reasons for this choice will be examined and analysed. The second focus will be on the representation of Mary and Pelagia in these texts, lead by the question if their femininity is actually preserved at all when they finally become pious brides of God.

Turning back to Adam and Eve, it is very simple to spot the guilty one after their expulsion from paradise. Of course it is Eve, the woman who could not resist temptation, who lead Adam on the wrong path and prevented every chance on an earthly paradise not just for herself, but for mankind. The assumption that women are not only incomplete copies of men but also the most sinful creatures on earth was a dominant one in Old English times. Among others, Herrin and Cox Miller point out that the term "holy woman" was a contradiction in terms. But if it is already hard to imagine a holy woman, how is it possible that a number of *harlots* have exactly reached that status, a status only ever given by men? Mary of Egypt can be seen as a prime example. She did not prostitute herself because she needed the money, she throws herself "entirely and insatiably into the lust of sexual intercourse", her lust is "a free gift". Yet instead of being utterly repelled, the monk Zosimas, who is actually looking for a "holy father", seems to see a holy mother in her. (Cf. Burrus).
First of all there is to say that these holy whores were certainly the "sexiest of saints" (ibid), an aspect which simply will have helped to make people read this Saint's Life. However, this entertainment purpose can not be the only reason for choosing such sinful ladies. Coon and Ward both emphasise the symbolic function of these harlots. Considering that everyone is ultimately a sinner, their lives remind the reader of their own sinful

state. And to achieve this, you do not write about an errant male, you write about the personification of sin: a female. Hence, Mary and Pelagia are "mediators of human salvation" (Coon).

What is striking here however, is the fact that the more pious and holy Mary and Pelagia become, the less feminine they seem to be portrayed. Due to their ascetic lives in the desert, their bodies loose all their female qualities. While Pelagia used to be known for her beauty, in the desert "her voluptuous flesh melts away to nothing [...] all that remains is the image of a skeleton loosely covered in skin as coarse as a sackcloth". (Burrus) Mary is similarly emaciated and her white hair rather reminds of a wise man than of a former harlot. Yet there is more evidence that suggests that Mary and Pelagia are represented in a masculine way. Mary is able to walk on water and has a "power of clairvoyance" which reminds of none other than Jesus Christ (cf. Coon). As mentioned before, her white hair seems like a symbol for her wisdom – obviously a male characteristic. Burrus further refers to the relation between Zosimas and Mary. Although Mary denies it, it is actually Zosimas who is her disciple; it is not the other way round. His reverence for her is obvious, for example when he urges her to tell him her life story. Thus, the fact that Mary serves as a teacher for him makes her seem more masculine, too. Despite the fact that Mary is naked when Zosimas sees her, her ascetic life has already emaciated her, it is therefore not surprising that Zosimas does not describe her appearance at greater length. Covering herself with his cloak, Burrus points out that Mary looks "virilely feminine" in this "semiclothed state".

An increasing masculinity is even more obvious in the case of Pelagia as she totally sheds her femininity by pretending to be a monk. Her transformation also seems more intense because the reader gets to know her as the bejewelled, beautiful courtesan. However, already at this stage there might be a first sign of her oncoming disguise. In this context Christine Rauer's essay on Pelagia's cloak ("byrne" in the original source) is interesting. Discussing several potential meanings, Rauer also translates "byrne" as a piece of war-clothing, suggesting this could refer to a symbolic protection. In my reading however, this can also be seen as a reference to masculinity, considering that Pelagia is about to travel towards her future as Pelagius. Furthermore Nonnus gives us a good idea of how Pelagia is perceived. The fact that he tells another monk to visit "Pelagius" and to benefit from his wisdom, suggests that Nonnus has accepted Pelagia in her new role. That he refers to her as an "eunuch" does not only mark her as a male, but also suggests that she is completely deprived of her sexuality. (Cf. Cox Miller).

Clark has said that there was "a tendency to position the identity of holy women in terms of male-gendered norms". In the case of Mary of Egypt and Pelagia these male-gendered norms are clearly visible, both women do not achieve their saintly status due to any female virtues; the contrary is the case.

In the beginning of this essay it was stated that a "holy woman" is a contradiction in terms. After examining Mary's and Pelagia's lives it has to be said that this contradiction could not be solved, it has rather been emphasised. As David points out "the identities of Mary and Pelagia are simultaneously affirmed and negated". They both "approach the holy, but their full embodiment of it is undermined by the gendered contradictions that cluster around them." (Cox Miller).